Draw with

ART FOR KIDS HUB

ANIMALS

30 step-by-step drawing projects inside!

Rob Jensen

DK

DK | Penguin Random House

Senior Designer Lauren Adams
Senior Production Editor Jennifer Murray
Senior Production Controller Louise Minihane
Senior Acquisitions Editor Pete Jorgensen
Managing Art Editor Jo Connor
Publishing Director Mark Searle
Written and Illustrated by Rob Jensen

Designed and Edited by Elizabeth T. Gilbert and Rebecca Razo
at Coffee Cup Creative, LLC.

Copyedited by Beth Adelman

First American Edition, 2024
Published in the United States by DK Publishing
1745 Broadway, 20th Floor, New York, NY 10019

Page design copyright © 2024 Dorling Kindersley Limited
DK, a Division of Penguin Random House LLC
24 25 26 27 28 10 9 8 7 6 5 4 3 2
002–339829–May/2024

© 2024 Art for Kids Hub

A catalog record for this book
is available from the Library of Congress.
ISBN 978-0-7440-9888-4

DK books are available at special discounts when purchased
in bulk for sales promotions, premiums, fund-raising, or educational use.
For details, contact: DK Publishing Special Markets,
1745 Broadway, 20th Floor, New York, NY 10019
SpecialSales@dk.com

Printed and bound in China

www.dk.com

www.artforkidshub.com

MIX
Paper | Supporting
responsible forestry
FSC™ C018179

This book was made with Forest
Stewardship Council™ certified
paper – one small step in DK's
commitment to a sustainable future.
Learn more at
www.dk.com/uk/information/sustainability

Draw with ART FOR KIDS HUB

ANIMALS

30 step-by-step drawing projects inside!

Rob Jensen

PART I: Step-by-Step Projects....16

Table of CONTENTS

PART II: You're an Artist!....78

Welcome to Art for Kids Hub!

Hey, friends! I'm Rob. And along with my amazing wife, Teryn, and our four creative kids, Jack, Hadley, Austin, and Olivia, we make art together as a family—and we love sharing it with you!

This book is divided into two parts. In Part I, you'll find step-by-step drawing lessons for a super cool collection of animals. Each drawing is ranked Level 1, Level 2, or Level 3 according to its difficulty (see the Symbol Key on the opposite page). Don't worry, though! You'll be able to draw all the animals by following along step by step.

In Part II, you'll find tips for drawing backgrounds, props, and completed scenes for your animals. I've also included some folding surprise drawing projects at the very end. Whether you're a beginner or a budding artist, there's something fun for everyone.

Ready to begin? Grab your art tools and some paper, and let's make art that brings smiles and creates joy!

ROB

TERYN

AUSTIN

JACK

OLIVIA

HADLEY

About This Book

For each project, follow the steps in red to complete your drawing. Then add color using your favorite art tools. It's as simple as that!

1

2

3

Symbol Key

Each project is marked with one of the following symbols, from less difficult to a little more challenging. But don't be afraid to try them all!

 = Level 1

 = Level 2

 = Level 3

 = Great work!

MORE IN THIS BOOK

☑ Draw trees, mountains, flowers, clouds, and other elements from nature.

☑ Combine drawings to make completed scenes and backgrounds.

☑ Create fun folding surprise drawings.

Art Tools & SUPPLIES

Here are some art tools you can use to draw and color the projects in this book. These are some of my favorite supplies, but you can use any tools that are available to you.

Black Marker

I like to draw with a permanent black marker for a bold, solid outline. But feel free to start your drawings with pencil if you prefer.

CHECKLIST

☑ A flat drawing surface, like a table or clipboard

☑ Marker paper

☑ Black permanent marker

☑ Pencil and sharpener

☑ Coloring tools, such as colored pencils, markers, and crayons

Paper

White marker paper is perfect if you're using markers to color, and regular paper is fine if you are using crayons or colored pencils.

Markers

Markers create smooth, solid strokes of color. Some sets include both fine tips and thick tips. I use alcohol-based markers because they dry quickly, and their colors don't fade easily.

Crayons

Wax crayons are inexpensive and easy to find. Sometimes they create a bumpy texture and can be hard to blend, so I use gel crayons. They are creamy and extra smooth.

Colored Pencils

These tools are clean and simple. You can even layer them to blend and shade. Keep a sharpener on hand for pointy tips.

Pastels

There are two types of pastels: soft pastels and oil pastels. Soft pastels feel like chalk and create smooth, light blends. Oil pastels feel more like crayons and create bold, bright strokes.

We would LOVE to see your drawings! Learn how to share them with us here.

Brushes

Brushes come in a range of sizes and shapes. Brushes with natural bristles are best for watercolor paints, and synthetic bristles are best for acrylics. When you've finished painting, rinse your brushes with soap and warm water, and reshape the bristles before they dry.

Paints

Watercolor, tempera, and acrylic paints are water-based media that you can use to color your art. Be sure to use them on sturdy paper, such as watercolor paper. While you paint, keep a cup of water nearby for rinsing your brushes—and have plenty of paper towels on hand for cleanup.

WATERCOLOR

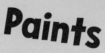

TEMPERA

ACRYLIC

Getting STARTED

Before you begin drawing, it's a great idea to warm up. From dots and swirls to dashes and curls, make all sorts of marks on scrap paper to get the creative juices flowing.

I use a lot of loops, dots, and curvy, squiggly, and jagged lines in my drawings. What other lines and scribbles can you make?

Basic Shapes

Most of the drawings in the book start with basic shapes like circles, triangles, squares, and ovals. Practice drawing these basic shapes and then draw new shapes of your own, if you like.

TRIANGLES

SQUARES, RECTANGLES & DIAMONDS

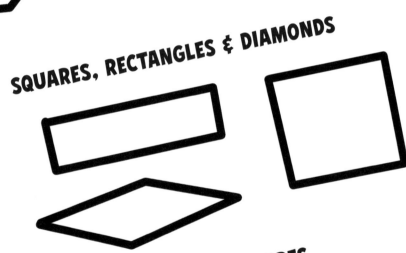

CIRCLES, OVALS, EGGS & BEAN SHAPES

The face reveals a character's emotions. In the examples below, see how the eyes, mouth, and other features can help you communicate feelings and personality.

A happy expression is my favorite, but it's fun to draw other emotions too.

HAPPY

SCARED

SILLY

ANGRY

SNEAKY

TIRED

EMBARRASSED

SWEET

EXCITED

All About COLOR

The Color Wheel

The color wheel is a visual aid for understanding how colors work together. The colors on this wheel are divided into two groups: primary (blue, yellow, red) and secondary (green, orange, purple).

Complementary Colors

Complementary colors are two colors that are opposite each other on the color wheel. When they're placed next to each other in a drawing or painting, they appear brighter. Some examples are yellow and purple, blue and orange, and red and green.

Color Temperature

Colors are divided into two temperatures: cool and warm. Blue, green, and purple are cool colors. Yellow, orange, and red are warm colors. Color temperature plays a part in the mood of a drawing. For example, cool colors are calm and warm colors are energetic.

WARM

COOL

Color Mixing

Every color combination begins with the primary colors. Secondary colors are made by mixing two primary colors. Yellow + red = orange, red + blue = purple, and blue + yellow = green. Gray is made by mixing white and black, while pink is made from a combination of white and red. White lightens colors; black darkens colors.

Coloring Steps

To bring your characters to life, try this three-step approach to adding color.

1

Add smooth, flat areas of color with your tools of choice.

2

Layer your colors—or use slightly darker shades—to create shadows.

3

Finish coloring your art by adding highlights with white.

I like to get creative with color in my drawings! How about you?

15

Part 1: STEP-BY-STEP PROJECTS

Hey, art friends!

To draw the animals in this section, start with Step 1 and continue to follow each new step in red. Along the way, you'll find lots of encouragement, helpful art tips, and even some fun animal facts.

I had so much fun creating these animal drawing lessons, but we especially love drawing together as a family. So, in addition to my drawings, you'll also see tons of great drawings by Teryn, Jack, Hadley, Austin, and Olivia. Each of us has our own art style, and we want to inspire you to draw in your own unique style, too. There are no mistakes and no wrong ways to make art—the important thing is to have fun and practice!

Happy creating!

Harry the HEDGEHOG

Begin with the eyes and a broad U shape for the body.

1

2

3

Add the feet, nails, and quills.

4

5

Be sure to add extras to your drawing! Check out Teryn's.

My hedgehog loves cookies!

Try This!

There are many ways to begin a drawing. One way is to look at the subject you want to draw and break it down into basic shapes, like a circle, an oval, or a letter shape—like U. How many basic shapes do you see in the hedgehog? Do they seem like easy shapes to draw?

Draw the face and the horn.

  1

 2

 **3**

Add the ears and draw the body.

 **4**

 **5**

 **6**

Continue to add the details to finish your drawing.

 **7**

 **8**

Try This!

Glittery gel pens and markers are ideal for adding color to this magical creature.

Kola the KOALA

Kola loves to hang in trees and eat leaves. In this drawing, I gave him a yummy snack.

Don't forget to share your koala drawing with us!

Begin with the nose, eyes, and face.

1

2

3

Continue to follow each new step in red.

4

5

6

Finish the ears and legs. Add a small tree branch.

7

8

9

Keep going! You've got this!

10

11

Artie the ARCTIC FOX

Draw the eyes, nose, ears, and chin.

1

2

3

Continue to follow each new step in red.

 **4**

5

6

Complete the details and add a bushy tail.

 **7**

8

DID YOU KNOW?
Arctic foxes often use the same den over many generations. Some dens are hundreds of years old and have multiple entrances, tunnels, and nests—a little city underground!

25

Donut the BUNNY

2

DID YOU KNOW?

In real life, bunnies like hay, leafy greens, and other veggies. But in the cartoon drawing world, anything goes. And this bunny loves a good donut with extra icing!

I think chocolate icing with rainbow sprinkles is the ultimate donut.

I colored my donut pink because I love strawberry icing.

26

Try This!

There are many kinds of donuts. What kind does your bunny like? Add those details to your drawing.

Begin with the eyes, nose, and face.

1

2

3

Continue to add the details and start the donut.

4

5

6

Finish the drawing. Don't forget the sprinkles!

7

8

3

Syd the SQUIRREL

Squirrels twitch their bushy tails to communicate with other squirrels. They also have a range of vocal chirps they use to "talk."

Let's begin with the face and the brim of the hat.

1

2

3

Follow the steps in red to complete the head and build the body. Then add to the hat.

4

5

6

Finish the hat, paws, and ears. Then start the tail.

7

8

9

Try This!

Add personality to your drawings with hats, bow ties, clothes, and other accessories.

Finish that bushy tail, the ears, and feet.

10

11

I colored the top hat ribbon gold.

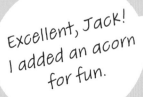

Excellent, Jack! I added an acorn for fun.

Pudgy the PANDA BEAR

Get creative with your drawing, if you like. I added a party hat to my panda!

My panda has a cute bow that matches her nose and feet!

Chip the CHIHUAHUA

Begin with the eyes, nose, and mouth. Add the head.

 1

 2

 3

Fill in the details, including the ears, body, and front legs.

4

 5

 6

Follow the steps in red to complete your drawing.

 7

 8

Give your pup a name to match its personality! I named my little guy "Chip."

I added a pink collar and a matching bow!

DID YOU KNOW?
The Chihuahua is the smallest dog breed by weight, height, and length, but it has one of the longest lifespans of all breeds—from 15 to 20 years, on average.

Try This!

Chihuahuas come in a variety of colors, including white, tan, brown, and black. Feel free to experiment using different color combinations on your pup!

Kangaroo JILL & BABY JOEY

Kangaroos in the wild are brown and tan, but Hadley got creative with her colors. What colors will you use?

DID YOU KNOW?
A female kangaroo is sometimes called a "jill" and a baby kangaroo is called a "joey." Joeys are about the size of a grape when they are born.

I can't wait to see your kangaroo drawing!

Let's begin with the face and an oval shape for the head.

1

2

3

Add eyelashes and a bow to this jill. Continue to add the details.

4

5

6

Finish the feet, tail, and joey to complete the drawing.

7

8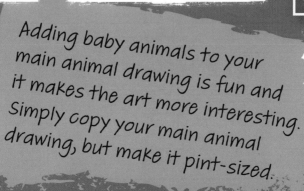

Adding baby animals to your main animal drawing is fun and it makes the art more interesting. Simply copy your main animal drawing, but make it pint-sized.

Try This!

Leonard the LION

Let's begin with the face.

1

2

3

Now add the mane and front legs.

4

5

6

Continue to follow each step in red.

7

8

9

Begin with the eyes, trunk, eyebrows, and face.

1

2

3

Complete the head, body, and ears. (Don't forget the tuft of hair!)

4

5

6

Follow the steps in red to add the details.

7

8

Try This!

There are a lot of shapes and lines in this drawing. Just take it one step at a time!

Dottie the GIRAFFE

I colored my giraffe yellow with brown spots. Great job, Teryn!

DID YOU KNOW?

No two giraffes are exactly alike! Each giraffe has its own unique spot pattern—it's kind of like human fingerprints.

Rob, I love your giraffe's blue eye.

Let's begin with the muzzle, eye, face, and horn. Then start the body.

1

2

3

Continue to follow the steps in red.

4

5

6

Finish the legs, tail, hooves, and spots.

7

8

Stripes the TIGER

Draw a half circle for the head. Then add the eyes and face.

1

2

3

Now add the ears, whiskers, and front legs.

4

5

6

Follow the steps in red to complete the details.

7

8

9

Try This!

Turn this tiger into a cheetah by replacing the stripes with spots.

Now add the stripes!

10

11

Add as many, or as few, stripes as you'd like.

I added a heart because my tiger is cute and cuddly!

Millie the MONKEY

That's a fantastic monkey, Olivia! Did you enjoy drawing it?

I did! But I changed my colors to green and blue.

Let's start with the eyes and nose. Then begin drawing the head.

1

2

3

Continue to draw the head, ears, and arms.

4

5

6

Great job! Keep going. You've got this!

7

8

Begin with the eyes in the middle of your paper. That way you'll have a lot of room to draw the head and body.

Try This!

45

Begin with the eye, muzzle, ear, and front part of the body.

1

2

3

Continue to draw the body and mane.

4

5

6

Finish the mane, legs, and tail.

7

8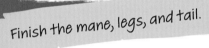

9

Hooray! Well done!

Try This!

Remember, your drawing doesn't have to look exactly like ours. The most important thing is to practice and have fun!

Sparky the DRAGON

Let's begin with the eyes and face.

1

2

3

Continue to follow the steps in red.

4

5

6

Now add all the fun dragon details to bring Sparky to life!

7

8

9

Try This!

I love to draw cute and happy faces, but you can change the expression to scary, surprised, or even silly!

Well done! That's a great dragon!

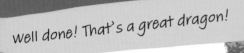

10

11

I colored the horns, scales, and webbing like fire.

I colored my dragon in different shades of green.

Finn the DOLPHIN

Begin with the eye and some curvy lines for the body and fin.

1

2

3

Keep following the steps in red to complete your drawing.

4

5

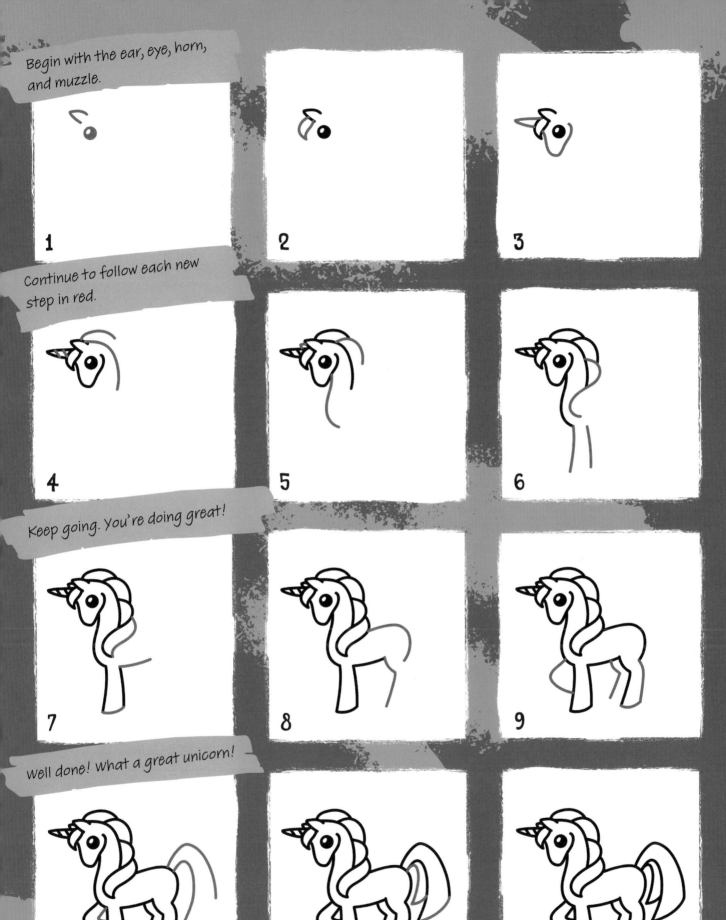

Begin with the ear, eye, horn, and muzzle.

1

2

3

Continue to follow each new step in red.

4

5

6

Keep going. You're doing great!

7

8

9

Well done! What a great unicorn!

10

11

Tony the T. REX

Begin with the eye and continue to follow the steps in red.

1

2

3

Now let's add some teeth and claws. Then start the body.

4

5

6

Look at that! You're almost done.

7

8

9

The meteor is a nice touch, Austin!

Thanks, Dad! I wonder what else I could add to the scene?

Add the stripes, scales, and toe claws to complete your drawing.

10

11

55

Let's begin with the face.

1

2

3

Now add some curvy lines to create the body.

4

5

6

Follow the steps in red to add the details.

7

8

9

Just a few minor additions will complete your drawing. Great work!

10

11

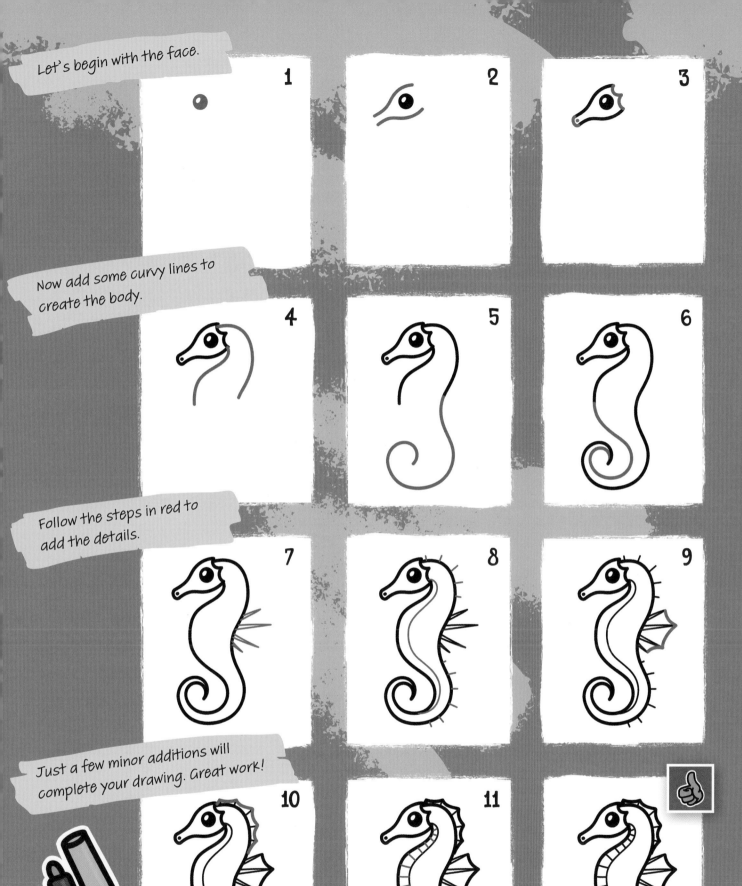

57

Pammy the OCTOPUS

Begin with the eyes, a circle for the head, and some curvy lines for the tentacles.

1

2

3

Keep following the steps in red.

4

5

6

Continue to draw the tentacles.

7

8

9

Use little half circles to add the suckers.

10

11

DID YOU KNOW?
The octopus has eight tentacles with strong suckers that it uses to grasp objects, explore its environment, and taste food!

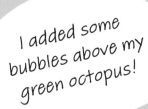

I added some bubbles above my green octopus!

I gave mine some red spots!

59

Let's begin with the eyes and a simple shape for the head.

1

2

3

Add the mouth and face details. Begin the body and flippers.

4

5

6

You're doing great! Keep on going!

7

8

9

Add the details to finish. Hooray!

10

11

Wally the NARWHAL

Great color combo on your narwhal, Hadley!

I like your bubbles, Dad! I might add some next time.

Follow each step in red to start the horn and face. Add the fin.

1

2

3

Now add a large C shape to complete the body. Begin the tail.

4

5

6

Add the final details to finish. Amazing job!

Try This!

Use long, sweeping strokes to create the narwhal's body.

7

Polly the PARROT

Let's start with the face. (Doesn't the first step look like a little stick man?)

1

2

3

Remember what to do? Follow the steps in red.

4

5

6

Complete the wings and other details.

7

8

Stuffy the TEDDY BEAR

I used traditional colors, but I did add some hearts around my bear.

I like white and purple for my bear.

Draw the nose, eyes, and mouth to begin.

1

2

3

This bear is made with a lot of curvy lines for the head, ears, and arms.

4

5

6

Continue to add the details, including a cute little bow tie.

7

8

Teddy bears come in a variety of colors, including brown, white, pink, and yellow. You can use any—or all—of your colors to make your teddy bear your own unique creation.

Try This!

67

Squeaky the BABY CHICK

You can draw Squeaky in just a few steps!
Begin with the eyes, beak, and head.

1

2

3

Add the body, wings, and feet. Great job!

4

5

What a cutie! Olivia, I love yours!

I made my chick brown and added a speckled egg.

Try This!

An upside-down triangle is perfect for this little chick's beak.

69

Let's draw some curvy lines for the eye, head, and body.

1

2

3

Add another curvy line for the wing, plus some straight lines for the legs.

4

5

6

Excellent job! Wasn't that fun?

7

Try This!

Red + White = Pink! If you don't have pink in your tools, you can color white over red for the same effect.

Plume the PEACOCK

Begin with the eye, beak, and a curvy line for the head.

1

2

3

Follow the steps in red to create the body and feathers.

4

5

6

Draw circles for the feather pattern and lines for the legs and feet.

7

8

Try This!

You can add any combination of blue, green, turquoise, purple, yellow, and orange to your drawing for an authentic color combo.

Peacock feathers are iridescent, which means the colors shift in the light. Those are great colors, Austin!

Next time, I'm going to try different shapes on the tail to make my own design.

Brenda the BUTTERFLY

Begin with the face and head.

1

2

3

Follow each step to create the body and wings.

4

5

6

Add some long loops for the wing details. Don't forget the antennae.

7

8

9

Try This!

Feel free to create your own pattern on the butterfly's wings using squiggly lines, circles, and swirls.

Finish the details to complete your drawing.

10

11

That's a great butterfly, Hadley!

Thanks! I made the wings really curvy.

Olive the OWL

DID YOU KNOW?
Owls have zygodactyl feet, which means they have two foward toes and two backward-facing toes!

I gave my owl a little perch to sit on.

I gave my owl extra-fluffy wings. Isn't she cute?

Let's begin with the face.

1

2

3

Next, add the ears, head, and some feathers.

4

5

6

Great work! Follow the rest of the steps in red to finish.

7

8

You can make your owl plump or skinny depending on where you place your lines. For a plump owl, draw the face lines in Step 3 farther apart. For a skinny owl, draw the face lines closer together.

Try This!

Part II: YOU'RE AN ARTIST!

In this section, you'll learn how to draw things that add interest to your art. I've also included instructions for creating two folding surprise drawings. Remember, there are no mistakes—your only goal is to have fun!

Symbols

Symbols can be used to express emotions, feelings, or a state of mind. For example, replacing a character's eyes with hearts suggests it might be thinking about love. Drawing sparkles around a unicorn gives it a magical feel. What other symbols could you add to your drawings?

BIG BOOM!
Use a big boom to show an explosion of thought, action, or excitement!

SPARKLES & HEARTS
Use sparkles to show something magical or dreamy. Hearts are great for showing affection and emphasizing cute things.

STARS & DIZZY LINES
Did your character bump its head? Use stars and dizzy lines to show confusion.

Speech Bubbles

Add personality to your characters with speech bubbles that show what they're saying or thinking.

Round and rectangular speech bubbles give your characters the ability to "talk" to each other or your readers.

This speech bubble is used to express enthusiasm or excitement!

This thought cloud reveals a character's internal thoughts to the reader.

what Olivia said.

Action & Movement

These fun details can add interest to your animal drawings by showing them in action.

FLYING

Swoosh! Did you feel that butterfly zip by?

SWIMMING

Splish-splash! This dolphin is having fun in the water.

BOUNCING

This little squirrel is boing...boing...boinging his way along.

FLOATING

Unicorn is floating high in the sky thanks to this puffy cloud shape.

LANDING

Ouch...Poor Teddy landed with a thud! Couldn't you just feel it?

RUNNING

Look at this pony run like the wind!

Props

Props are things like hats, glasses, toys, and other objects that add character, style, and a sense of place to your drawings. What other props can you think of to add to your creations?

SKATEBOARD

SUNGLASSES

DOG HOUSE

FOOD BOWL

The Great OUTDOORS

Every animal has a habitat—a place in nature where it lives. What other outdoor elements would you like to draw?

Trees

Use a cloud shape for this treetop.

Begin a tree with the trunk and then add your own shape for the top.

This treetop starts with a triangle.

Use a swirl for this rosebud.

Use circles and semicircles to draw the daisy.

Flowers

Layer leaf shapes with pointed tips for a tulip.

Use zigzags for grass.

Clouds

Use connected curves
for puffy clouds.

Sun

Draw the sun using a
circle and add zigzag
lines for the rays.

Moon & Stars

Use a backward C shape
to draw a crescent moon.

Mountains

Mountains can have pointed tops or rounded tops.

Volcano

A flat top, cloud shape, and squiggly line show this volcano erupting.

Ocean Waves

Sweeping and curvy lines are great for showing the ocean and waves.

Look how you can pull all the individual pieces together to form completed scenes. What other scenes would you like to draw?

Shredding Monkey

Nervous Dinosaur

Beachy Vibes

Fox in the Forest

Folding SURPRISE DRAWINGS

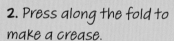

A folding surprise drawing is exactly what it sounds like: a drawing on folded paper that opens to reveal a surprise inside! This project is a lot of fun and gives an opportunity to stretch your creativity.

Before you begin, you'll need to prepare your paper so the surprise works the way it should. I used a sheet of printer paper (8.5" x 11"), but you can use any size paper you like.

Paper Set Up

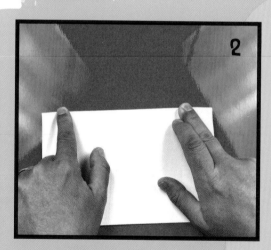

1. Lay the paper flat with the short sides of the paper on the top and bottom, and the long sides of the paper on the left and right. Fold the paper in half, lining up the top edge with the bottom edge.

2. Press along the fold to make a crease.

3. Gently lift the top flap of the paper.

4. Fold the top flap up, bringing the bottom edge to line up with the top edge. Press along the fold to make another crease.

5. and 6. Lift the paper and flip it over from right to left, so that the unfolded bottom flap is now on the top.

7. Lift the flap and fold it up to meet the top edge, repeating step 4.

8. Open the last fold you just made.

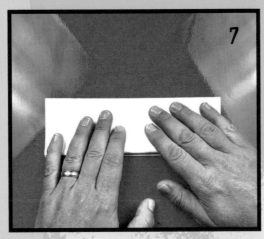

9. Flip your paper over from left to right, so it's back to the original side.

10. Your paper is now ready for your drawing! You will start the outside drawing on the folded paper.

Note: When you unfold the page, you should have four sections marked by folds.

Turn the page to get started on the first surprise drawing!

Hungry Shark

Follow the instructions for drawing on the folded paper. Open up the paper to complete drawing the surprise inside.

1

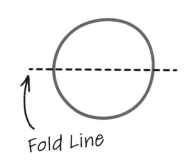

Fold Line

FOLDED

1. Place paper with the folded side up (see step 10 on page 89). Draw a circle so the fold line is dividing it in half.

2. Draw the eyes above the fold.

3. Draw the nostrils and the fin.

4. Add two more fins to the body.

2

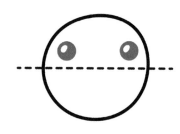

3

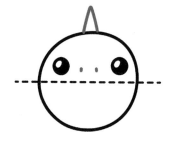

4

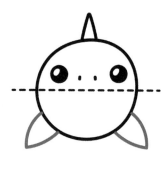

OPENED

1. Unfold your paper. You will see the face above the top fold and the body below the bottom fold.

2. Draw two parallel lines connecting the shark's head to the body.

3. Draw a large rectangle for the shark's mouth.

4. Add sharp teeth using zigzag lines.

5. Draw a tongue. (Sharks don't have tongues, but this is a cartoon—we can be creative!)

6. Finish the drawing with the shark's throat. Your shark is ready for a snack!

Turn the page to see how I added color to this bad boy!

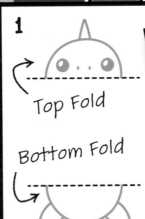

1

Top Fold

Bottom Fold

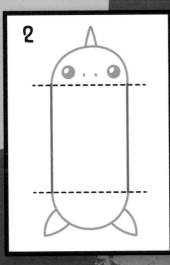

2

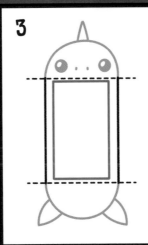

3

4

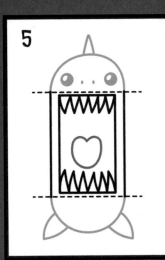

5

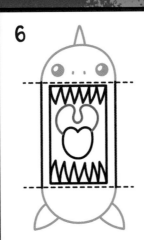

6

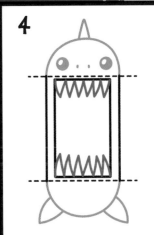

Try This!

Folding surprise drawings are fun to play with! After you've colored in your drawing, hold the top of the paper in one hand and the bottom of the paper in the other. Then move the paper to open and close the mouth to show the shark in action!

1. Refold the paper so only the outside drawing is visible; then add color.

1

2. Open the paper. Color the inside of the shark's mouth. I used dark red for inside the mouth, pink for the tongue, and black for the back of the throat.

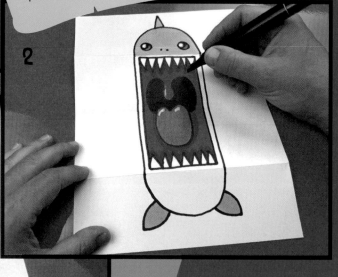

2

3. Add some fish around the shark's mouth. Looks like he's about to have a tasty snack!

3

Puppy Stack

3

FOLDED

1. Place the paper with the folded side up (see step 10 on page 89). Draw the eyes above the fold line and a half circle to start the head.

2. Draw two curved lines above the eyes and a small upside-down triangle for the nose.

3. Complete the face. Draw two zigzag lines for the front legs.

4. Add the ears, tongue, and paws.

5. Connect the ears. Draw two more lines for the back legs. Add the nails.

6. Draw the back legs and the ear details.

7. Add the tail and finishing touches.

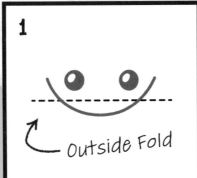

Outside Fold

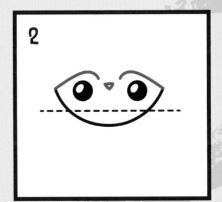

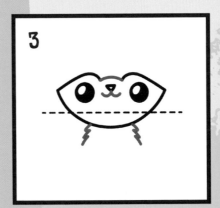

1

2

3

4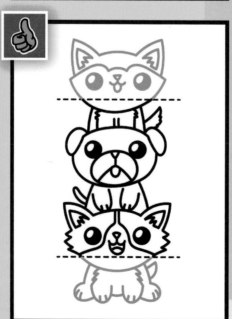

5

OPENED

1. Draw a large oval about a pinky finger's width below the top fold line. Add a smaller oval for the muzzle. Draw the ears. Draw the outline of the third puppy's head.

2. Draw the faces.

3. Complete the head of the top puppy. Draw the second puppy's body and the third puppy's mouth.

4. Draw the first puppy's body. Add U shapes for the second puppy's paws. Add the details to the third puppy.

5. Finish the legs, tails, nails, and ears.

ABOUT THE ARTIST

Rob Jensen, the fun-loving creator of Art for Kids Hub, has a background in industrial design, which fuels his passion for teaching art. He believes that creativity adds happiness and interest to life. Rob, along with his family, embodies the spirit of making art both easy and exciting. Collectively, the Jensens demonstrate that art is not just a solo journey but a shared family adventure. Together, they show the world how to create art in simple, engaging ways, one drawing at a time.

ABOUT ART FOR KIDS HUB

Art for Kids Hub is a family driven platform that brings the joy of art to families around the world. Co-created by Rob Jensen and his family, it offers a friendly, welcoming space for kids of all ages to learn and grow artistically. Recognized by various media outlets, Art for Kids Hub provides a diverse range of resources, including an engaging website, an online shop, and social media content full of art lessons. This platform is committed to making learning art fun and accessible, showcasing that art can be a delightful experience for everyone. It complements traditional art teaching by adding its unique, family oriented touch. Visit artforkidshub.com.

SOME WORDS OF GRATITUDE

In the creation of this book, I've been surrounded by an incredible circle of support and inspiration, each person contributing uniquely to this journey.

To Teryn, my wife and partner in everything: Your love, support, and friendship are the cornerstones of not only this book but of all our endeavors. I am endlessly grateful for your presence in my life. You make everything possible.

My deepest gratitude also goes to our children—Jack, Hadley, Austin, and Olivia. Your creativity, laughter, and shared joy in art have been the foundation of not only this book but all we do at Art for Kids Hub. You are my heart and inspiration.

A heartfelt thank you to DK, my publisher, for believing in this project. Pete Jorgensen, who first reached out to me with this wonderful opportunity: Your confidence in my work has been a great honor. Working with DK has been an enriching and fulfilling experience.

Special appreciation goes to Rebecca Razo and Elizabeth Gilbert at Coffee Cup Creative, LLC. Your expertise and vision have been instrumental in bringing this book to life. Your dedication and skill have transformed my ideas into something tangible and beautiful.

To my parents, Greg and Ruth Jensen, thank you for your unwavering encouragement and support since my childhood. Your belief in my passion for drawing has been a guiding light throughout my life and career.

I am also profoundly grateful to the young artists and their families who have joined us on Art for Kids Hub. Your enthusiasm and creativity have been a continuous source of inspiration and joy.

To the broader community of educators, fellow artists, and supporters, thank you for your encouragement and invaluable feedback. You have helped foster a nurturing space for young artists to thrive.

This book is a tribute to all of you. Your support, in so many ways, has made this journey an enriching and joyous adventure. Thank you for being part of our art family!

Rob Jensen